Seb and Mits

By Debbie Croft

Seb the cat
sat at the mat.

Tim ran to Seb.

Tim pats Seb.

Tim can see Mits.

Mits sits at the tap.

Mits can see Seb!

Mits ran at Seb the cat.

Seb ran!

Mits sat.

Seb sat.

Tim pats Mits.

Pat, pat, pat.

CHECKING FOR MEANING

1. Who is playing in the garden in the story? *(Literal)*

2. Where does Mits sit? *(Literal)*

3. Why do you think Tim pats Mits? *(Inferential)*

EXTENDING VOCABULARY

cat	Look at the word *cat*. Can you think of other words that rhyme with *cat*?
pats	Look at the word *pats*. What is the base of this word? What has been added to the base? Can you think of another word that has a similar meaning?
tap	What is the meaning of the word *tap* in this story? Can you think of another meaning for the word *tap*?

MOVING BEYOND THE TEXT

1. How do you think Seb and Mits feel when they see each other? Why?

2. Can you think of a time when you played with a pet or a friend? How did it make you feel?

3. How might the story be different if Seb and Mits were different animals?

SPEED SOUNDS

Cc	Bb	Rr	Ee	Ff	Hh	Nn
Mm	Ss	Aa	Pp	Ii	Tt	

PRACTICE WORDS

Seb

cat

ran

can